50 Premium Charcoal Recipes

By: Kelly Johnson

Table of Contents

- Charcoal-Grilled Wagyu Steak
- Smoky Charcoal-Roasted Lobster Tail
- Charcoal-Grilled Tomahawk Steak
- Miso-Glazed Charcoal-Grilled Black Cod
- Charcoal-Smoked Duck Breast
- Fire-Grilled Spanish Octopus
- Charcoal-Roasted Peking Duck
- Smoked Bourbon-Glazed Pork Ribs
- Charcoal-Grilled Bone Marrow
- Blackened Charcoal-Grilled Red Snapper
- Charcoal-Seared A5 Wagyu Striploin
- Charcoal-Roasted Garlic and Herb Chicken
- Honey-Glazed Charcoal-Grilled Lamb Chops
- Charcoal-Baked Potatoes with Truffle Butter
- Smoked Charcoal-Roasted Corn on the Cob
- Charcoal-Grilled Pineapple with Rum Glaze
- Fire-Roasted Whole Branzino
- Smoked Charcoal-Brined Turkey Breast
- Charcoal-Seared Scallops with Lemon Butter
- Charcoal-Grilled Mediterranean Eggplant
- Charcoal-Roasted Chestnuts with Sea Salt
- Tandoori-Style Charcoal-Grilled Chicken
- Blackened Charcoal-Seared Tuna Steak
- Slow-Smoked Charcoal Beef Brisket
- Charcoal-Roasted Sweet Potatoes with Miso Glaze
- Charcoal-Baked Flatbread with Za'atar
- Fire-Grilled Lobster with Garlic Butter
- Smoked Charcoal-Grilled Pork Belly
- Charcoal-Grilled Bone-In Ribeye
- Fire-Kissed Charcoal-Grilled Oysters
- Smoky Charcoal-Roasted Portobello Mushrooms
- Charcoal-Seared Duck Breast with Plum Sauce
- Charcoal-Grilled Spicy Chorizo
- Blackened Cajun Charcoal-Grilled Shrimp
- Smoked Charcoal-Roasted Baby Back Ribs

- Charcoal-Grilled Wagyu Burgers with Truffle Aioli
- Charcoal-Smoked Maple-Glazed Salmon
- Charcoal-Baked Camembert with Honey
- Smoked Charcoal-Roasted Pork Shoulder
- Fire-Grilled Asparagus with Lemon Zest
- Smoked Charcoal-Brined Short Ribs
- Charcoal-Seared Filet Mignon with Herb Butter
- Charcoal-Roasted Wild Mushrooms with Garlic
- Charcoal-Smoked Duck Confit
- Fire-Kissed Charcoal-Grilled Halloumi
- Blackened Charcoal-Seared Swordfish Steak
- Charcoal-Baked Stuffed Bell Peppers
- Charcoal-Grilled Clams with White Wine Sauce
- Smoked Charcoal-Roasted Beet Salad
- Charcoal-Grilled Tandoori Paneer

Charcoal-Grilled Wagyu Steak

Ingredients:

- 12 oz A5 Wagyu steak
- 1 tsp sea salt
- ½ tsp black pepper
- 1 tbsp olive oil

Instructions:

1. Let Wagyu come to room temperature.
2. Preheat charcoal grill to high heat.
3. Lightly brush steak with olive oil and season with salt and pepper.
4. Sear for 1-2 minutes per side for a rare center.
5. Rest for 5 minutes before slicing.

Smoky Charcoal-Roasted Lobster Tail

Ingredients:

- 2 lobster tails
- 4 tbsp butter, melted
- 1 tbsp smoked paprika
- 2 cloves garlic, minced
- Juice of ½ lemon

Instructions:

1. Butterfly lobster tails and brush with butter, paprika, and garlic.
2. Roast over medium charcoal heat for 5-7 minutes, basting occasionally.
3. Squeeze lemon juice over before serving.

Charcoal-Grilled Tomahawk Steak

Ingredients:

- 1 tomahawk steak (2-3 lbs)
- 2 tbsp kosher salt
- 1 tbsp cracked black pepper
- 2 tbsp butter

Instructions:

1. Season steak and let it rest at room temperature for 1 hour.
2. Grill over indirect charcoal heat (250°F) for 45 minutes until internal temp reaches 120°F.
3. Sear directly over high heat for 2 minutes per side.
4. Rest for 10 minutes before slicing.

Miso-Glazed Charcoal-Grilled Black Cod

Ingredients:

- 2 black cod fillets
- 3 tbsp white miso paste
- 1 tbsp mirin
- 1 tbsp sake
- 1 tbsp sugar

Instructions:

1. Mix miso, mirin, sake, and sugar, then marinate cod for 24 hours.
2. Grill over medium charcoal heat until caramelized (about 5 minutes per side).

Charcoal-Smoked Duck Breast

Ingredients:

- 2 duck breasts
- 1 tsp kosher salt
- 1 tsp Chinese five-spice
- ½ tsp black pepper

Instructions:

1. Score duck skin and season.
2. Sear skin-side down over indirect charcoal heat for 10 minutes.
3. Flip and cook for another 5 minutes until internal temp reaches 130°F.

Fire-Grilled Spanish Octopus

Ingredients:

- 1 octopus (2-3 lbs), pre-boiled
- 2 tbsp olive oil
- 1 tsp smoked paprika
- 1 tsp sea salt

Instructions:

1. Toss boiled octopus in olive oil, paprika, and salt.
2. Grill over high heat until lightly charred (about 3 minutes per side).

Charcoal-Roasted Peking Duck

Ingredients:

- 1 whole duck
- 2 tbsp hoisin sauce
- 1 tbsp soy sauce
- 1 tbsp honey
- 2 cloves garlic, minced

Instructions:

1. Coat duck in hoisin, soy sauce, honey, and garlic.
2. Hang or place over indirect charcoal heat and roast for 1.5-2 hours at 300°F.

Smoked Bourbon-Glazed Pork Ribs

Ingredients:

- 1 rack pork ribs
- ½ cup bourbon
- ¼ cup brown sugar
- 2 tbsp soy sauce
- 1 tsp smoked paprika

Instructions:

1. Smoke ribs at 250°F for 3 hours using charcoal and wood chips.
2. Glaze with bourbon, sugar, soy sauce, and paprika, then cook for another hour.

Charcoal-Grilled Bone Marrow

Ingredients:

- 4 beef marrow bones, cut lengthwise
- 1 tsp sea salt
- 1 tbsp parsley, chopped

Instructions:

1. Grill marrow bones over medium heat for 15 minutes until bubbling.
2. Sprinkle with salt and parsley before serving.

Blackened Charcoal-Grilled Red Snapper

Ingredients:

- 2 red snapper fillets
- 1 tbsp Cajun seasoning
- 2 tbsp butter, melted

Instructions:

1. Rub fish with Cajun seasoning and butter.
2. Grill over high heat for 3-4 minutes per side.

Charcoal-Seared A5 Wagyu Striploin

Ingredients:

- 12 oz A5 Wagyu striploin
- 1 tsp flaky sea salt
- 1 tsp black pepper

Instructions:

1. Sear over blazing hot charcoal for 1-2 minutes per side.
2. Let rest before slicing.

Charcoal-Roasted Garlic and Herb Chicken

Ingredients:

- 1 whole chicken (3-4 lbs)
- 3 tbsp olive oil
- 1 tbsp kosher salt
- 1 tbsp black pepper
- 4 cloves garlic, minced
- 1 tbsp fresh rosemary, chopped
- 1 tbsp thyme, chopped

Instructions:

1. Rub chicken with oil, salt, pepper, garlic, rosemary, and thyme.
2. Set up a charcoal grill for indirect heat (about 325°F).
3. Roast for 1.5-2 hours, turning occasionally, until internal temp reaches 165°F.

Honey-Glazed Charcoal-Grilled Lamb Chops

Ingredients:

- 8 lamb chops
- 2 tbsp honey
- 1 tbsp soy sauce
- 1 tbsp Dijon mustard
- 1 tsp black pepper

Instructions:

1. Mix honey, soy sauce, mustard, and pepper, then marinate lamb for 1 hour.
2. Grill over high charcoal heat for 3-4 minutes per side.

Charcoal-Baked Potatoes with Truffle Butter

Ingredients:

- 4 russet potatoes
- 2 tbsp truffle butter
- 1 tsp sea salt

Instructions:

1. Wrap potatoes in foil and place directly in hot charcoal.
2. Bake for 45-60 minutes, rotating occasionally.
3. Slice open and top with truffle butter.

Smoked Charcoal-Roasted Corn on the Cob

Ingredients:

- 4 ears of corn
- 2 tbsp butter, melted
- 1 tsp smoked paprika
- ½ tsp sea salt

Instructions:

1. Brush corn with butter, paprika, and salt.
2. Wrap in foil and place over indirect charcoal heat for 20-25 minutes.

Charcoal-Grilled Pineapple with Rum Glaze

Ingredients:

- 1 pineapple, sliced into rings
- ¼ cup dark rum
- 2 tbsp brown sugar
- 1 tsp cinnamon

Instructions:

1. Mix rum, sugar, and cinnamon.
2. Brush over pineapple and grill over high heat for 2 minutes per side.

Fire-Roasted Whole Branzino

Ingredients:

- 1 whole branzino, cleaned
- 2 tbsp olive oil
- 1 lemon, sliced
- 2 cloves garlic, minced
- 1 tsp sea salt

Instructions:

1. Stuff fish with lemon and garlic, then brush with olive oil and salt.
2. Grill over medium charcoal heat for 4-5 minutes per side.

Smoked Charcoal-Brined Turkey Breast

Ingredients:

- 1 turkey breast (2-3 lbs)
- ¼ cup kosher salt
- 4 cups water
- 1 tbsp black pepper
- 1 tbsp smoked paprika

Instructions:

1. Dissolve salt in water, add turkey, and brine for 12 hours.
2. Smoke over low charcoal heat (250°F) for 2-3 hours.

Charcoal-Seared Scallops with Lemon Butter

Ingredients:

- 8 large scallops
- 2 tbsp butter
- Juice of ½ lemon
- ½ tsp sea salt

Instructions:

1. Heat a cast-iron pan over charcoal.
2. Sear scallops in butter for 1-2 minutes per side.
3. Finish with lemon juice.

Charcoal-Grilled Mediterranean Eggplant

Ingredients:

- 2 eggplants, sliced
- 2 tbsp olive oil
- 1 tsp sea salt
- 1 tsp oregano

Instructions:

1. Brush eggplant with oil, salt, and oregano.
2. Grill over medium heat for 3-4 minutes per side.

Charcoal-Roasted Chestnuts with Sea Salt

Ingredients:

- 1 lb fresh chestnuts
- 1 tsp sea salt

Instructions:

1. Score chestnuts with an "X" and place in foil.
2. Roast in hot charcoal for 15-20 minutes, shaking occasionally.

Tandoori-Style Charcoal-Grilled Chicken

Ingredients:

- 4 bone-in, skin-on chicken thighs
- ½ cup plain yogurt
- 1 tbsp lemon juice
- 1 tbsp garam masala
- 1 tsp paprika
- 1 tsp turmeric
- 1 tsp cumin
- 1 tbsp grated ginger
- 2 cloves garlic, minced
- 1 tsp salt

Instructions:

1. Mix yogurt, lemon juice, and spices into a marinade.
2. Coat chicken and marinate for **6-12 hours**.
3. Grill over **medium-high charcoal heat** for **6-7 minutes per side**.

Blackened Charcoal-Seared Tuna Steak

Ingredients:

- 2 tuna steaks (6 oz each)
- 1 tbsp olive oil
- 1 tsp smoked paprika
- ½ tsp cayenne pepper
- 1 tsp black pepper
- ½ tsp sea salt

Instructions:

1. Coat tuna steaks with oil and spice mix.
2. Sear on **high charcoal heat** for **1 minute per side** for rare.

Slow-Smoked Charcoal Beef Brisket

Ingredients:

- 5 lb beef brisket
- 2 tbsp kosher salt
- 1 tbsp black pepper
- 1 tbsp smoked paprika
- 1 tbsp garlic powder
- 1 tbsp brown sugar

Instructions:

1. Rub brisket with spices and **rest for 1 hour**.
2. Smoke over **low heat (225°F)** for **10-12 hours**, wrapping in foil at the 6-hour mark.
3. Let it **rest for 1 hour** before slicing.

Charcoal-Roasted Sweet Potatoes with Miso Glaze

Ingredients:

- 4 sweet potatoes
- 2 tbsp white miso paste
- 1 tbsp honey
- 1 tbsp soy sauce
- 1 tsp sesame oil

Instructions:

1. Wrap sweet potatoes in foil and **roast in hot charcoal** for **45-60 minutes**.
2. Mix miso, honey, soy sauce, and sesame oil, then brush over cooked potatoes.

Charcoal-Baked Flatbread with Za'atar

Ingredients:

- 2 cups flour
- 1 tsp salt
- ¾ cup water
- 1 tbsp olive oil
- 1 tbsp za'atar seasoning

Instructions:

1. Mix flour, salt, water, and oil into a dough, let rest for **30 minutes**.
2. Roll out and grill over **medium heat** for **2-3 minutes per side**.
3. Brush with oil and sprinkle with za'atar.

Fire-Grilled Lobster with Garlic Butter

Ingredients:

- 2 whole lobsters, halved
- ¼ cup butter, melted
- 2 cloves garlic, minced
- 1 tbsp lemon juice

Instructions:

1. Mix butter, garlic, and lemon juice.
2. Grill lobsters **shell-side down** over high charcoal heat for **5-6 minutes**.
3. Brush with garlic butter before serving.

Smoked Charcoal-Grilled Pork Belly

Ingredients:

- 2 lbs pork belly, skin scored
- 1 tbsp sea salt
- 1 tbsp smoked paprika
- 1 tsp black pepper
- 1 tbsp soy sauce

Instructions:

1. Rub pork belly with spices and **marinate for 4 hours**.
2. Smoke over **low charcoal heat (250°F)** for **3-4 hours** until crispy.

Charcoal-Grilled Bone-In Ribeye

Ingredients:

- 1 bone-in ribeye (16 oz)
- 1 tbsp sea salt
- 1 tbsp black pepper
- 1 tbsp olive oil
- 1 tbsp butter

Instructions:

1. Season steak and let it rest at room temperature for **30 minutes**.
2. Sear over **high charcoal heat** for **3-4 minutes per side**, then **rest for 10 minutes** before slicing.

Fire-Kissed Charcoal-Grilled Oysters

Ingredients:

- 12 fresh oysters
- ¼ cup butter, melted
- 2 cloves garlic, minced
- 1 tbsp lemon juice
- 1 tsp hot sauce

Instructions:

1. Shuck oysters and place on the grill.
2. Drizzle with butter mixture and grill for **3-4 minutes** until bubbling.

Smoky Charcoal-Roasted Portobello Mushrooms

Ingredients:

- 4 large portobello mushrooms
- 2 tbsp balsamic vinegar
- 1 tbsp olive oil
- 1 tsp sea salt
- ½ tsp black pepper

Instructions:

1. Brush mushrooms with oil, vinegar, salt, and pepper.
2. Grill over **medium heat** for **4-5 minutes per side**.

Charcoal-Seared Duck Breast with Plum Sauce

Ingredients:

- 2 duck breasts, skin scored
- 1 tsp sea salt
- ½ tsp black pepper
- 1 tbsp olive oil

Plum Sauce:

- 4 ripe plums, pitted and chopped
- 2 tbsp honey
- 1 tbsp soy sauce
- 1 tsp ginger, grated

Instructions:

1. **Preheat grill to medium-high heat.**
2. **Season duck** with salt and pepper.
3. **Sear skin-side down for 4-5 min** until crispy.
4. Flip and cook for **3-4 min** until medium-rare.
5. **Simmer plums, honey, soy sauce, and ginger** for 5 minutes, then blend.
6. Slice duck and serve with plum sauce.

Charcoal-Grilled Spicy Chorizo

Ingredients:

- 4 chorizo sausages
- 1 tbsp olive oil
- 1 tsp smoked paprika
- 1 tsp chili flakes

Instructions:

1. Coat chorizo with olive oil, paprika, and chili flakes.
2. Grill over **medium heat for 8-10 minutes**, turning frequently.

🔥 **Pro Tip:** Serve with crusty bread and chimichurri!

Blackened Cajun Charcoal-Grilled Shrimp

Ingredients:

- 1 lb large shrimp, peeled & deveined
- 1 tbsp Cajun seasoning
- 1 tbsp olive oil
- 1 tbsp butter, melted
- 1 tsp smoked paprika

Instructions:

1. Toss shrimp in **oil and Cajun seasoning.**
2. Grill over **high heat** for **2-3 minutes per side.**
3. Drizzle with **melted butter & paprika.**

🔥 **Best served with a squeeze of fresh lime!**

Smoked Charcoal-Roasted Baby Back Ribs

Ingredients:

- 2 racks baby back ribs
- 1 tbsp salt
- 1 tbsp black pepper
- 1 tbsp smoked paprika
- 1 tbsp brown sugar
- 1 tsp garlic powder

Instructions:

1. Rub ribs with seasoning and let sit for **1 hour.**
2. **Smoke at 225°F for 5-6 hours,** wrapping in foil after 3 hours.
3. Glaze with BBQ sauce and sear over high heat for **5 min.**

Charcoal-Grilled Wagyu Burgers with Truffle Aioli

Ingredients:

- 1 lb Wagyu ground beef
- 1 tsp salt
- ½ tsp black pepper
- 4 brioche buns

Truffle Aioli:

- ½ cup mayo
- 1 tsp truffle oil
- ½ tsp garlic powder

Instructions:

1. Form beef into patties and season with salt & pepper.
2. Grill over **medium-high heat for 3-4 min per side.**
3. Mix truffle aioli and spread over toasted buns.

Charcoal-Smoked Maple-Glazed Salmon

Ingredients:

- 2 salmon fillets
- ¼ cup maple syrup
- 1 tbsp soy sauce
- 1 tsp Dijon mustard
- 1 tsp smoked salt

Instructions:

1. Mix maple syrup, soy sauce, mustard, and salt.
2. Brush over salmon and let marinate **for 30 min.**
3. Smoke at **225°F for 1 hour** or grill over medium heat for **5 min per side.**

Charcoal-Baked Camembert with Honey

Ingredients:

- 1 whole Camembert cheese
- 1 tbsp honey
- 1 tsp rosemary
- 1 tsp crushed walnuts

Instructions:

1. **Wrap Camembert in foil** and place on grill over **medium heat for 10 min.**
2. Drizzle with honey, rosemary, and walnuts.

Smoked Charcoal-Roasted Pork Shoulder

Ingredients:

- 5 lb pork shoulder
- 1 tbsp salt
- 1 tbsp black pepper
- 1 tbsp brown sugar
- 1 tsp smoked paprika

Instructions:

1. **Rub pork with seasoning and let sit overnight.**
2. Smoke at **225°F for 8-10 hours** until tender.
3. Let rest for **1 hour**, then shred and serve.

Fire-Grilled Asparagus with Lemon Zest

Ingredients:

- 1 bunch asparagus
- 1 tbsp olive oil
- ½ tsp sea salt
- 1 tsp lemon zest

Instructions:

1. Toss asparagus with oil and salt.
2. Grill over **medium-high heat for 3-4 minutes.**
3. Sprinkle with **lemon zest before serving.**

Smoked Charcoal-Brined Short Ribs

Ingredients:

- 4 lbs beef short ribs
- ¼ cup sea salt
- ¼ cup brown sugar
- 1 tbsp black pepper
- 1 tbsp smoked paprika
- 2 tbsp apple cider vinegar
- 1 tbsp Worcestershire sauce

Instructions:

1. **Brine ribs in salt, sugar, and water overnight.**
2. Pat dry and rub with pepper, paprika, and Worcestershire sauce.
3. **Smoke at 225°F for 5-6 hours** until tender.
4. **Finish over high heat for 2-3 minutes per side.**

Charcoal-Seared Filet Mignon with Herb Butter

Ingredients:

- 2 filet mignon steaks (6 oz each)
- 1 tbsp olive oil
- 1 tsp sea salt
- ½ tsp black pepper

Herb Butter:

- 2 tbsp butter
- 1 tsp chopped parsley
- 1 tsp chopped thyme
- ½ tsp minced garlic

Instructions:

1. Rub steaks with oil, salt, and pepper.
2. Sear over **high heat for 3-4 minutes per side.**
3. Rest for **5 minutes**, then top with herb butter.

Charcoal-Roasted Wild Mushrooms with Garlic

Ingredients:

- 2 cups mixed wild mushrooms
- 1 tbsp olive oil
- 1 tsp sea salt
- ½ tsp black pepper
- 1 tsp minced garlic
- 1 tbsp balsamic vinegar

Instructions:

1. Toss mushrooms in **olive oil, salt, and garlic.**
2. Grill in a cast-iron pan over **medium heat for 5 minutes.**
3. Finish with balsamic vinegar.

Charcoal-Smoked Duck Confit

Ingredients:

- 2 duck legs
- 1 tbsp sea salt
- 1 tsp black pepper
- 1 tbsp fresh thyme
- 2 cloves garlic, minced
- 1 tbsp duck fat

Instructions:

1. Rub duck with salt, pepper, and thyme.
2. Slow-cook in duck fat at **225°F for 3 hours**.
3. Smoke over charcoal for **10 minutes per side**.

Fire-Kissed Charcoal-Grilled Halloumi

Ingredients:

- 8 oz halloumi cheese, sliced
- 1 tbsp olive oil
- ½ tsp smoked paprika
- ½ tsp black pepper
- 1 tsp lemon zest

Instructions:

1. Brush halloumi with olive oil and seasonings.
2. Grill over **medium heat for 1-2 minutes per side** until golden.
3. Finish with lemon zest.

Blackened Charcoal-Seared Swordfish Steak

Ingredients:

- 2 swordfish steaks
- 1 tbsp olive oil
- 1 tsp Cajun seasoning
- ½ tsp smoked paprika
- 1 tsp lemon juice

Instructions:

1. Coat swordfish in **oil, Cajun seasoning, and paprika.**
2. Grill over **high heat for 4 minutes per side.**
3. Finish with **fresh lemon juice.**

Charcoal-Baked Stuffed Bell Peppers

Ingredients:

- 4 bell peppers, halved
- 1 cup cooked quinoa or rice
- ½ lb ground beef or lentils
- 1 tsp smoked paprika
- ½ tsp salt
- ½ tsp black pepper
- ½ cup shredded cheese

Instructions:

1. Mix filling ingredients and stuff into bell peppers.
2. Wrap in foil and bake over **medium heat for 15-20 minutes.**
3. Remove foil and grill for **2-3 minutes** to char edges.

Charcoal-Grilled Clams with White Wine Sauce

Ingredients:

- 2 lbs fresh clams
- 2 tbsp butter
- ½ cup white wine
- 2 cloves garlic, minced
- 1 tbsp chopped parsley

Instructions:

1. Grill clams over **high heat** until they open.
2. Melt butter and sauté garlic, then add white wine.
3. Pour sauce over clams and sprinkle with parsley.

Smoked Charcoal-Roasted Beet Salad

Ingredients:

- 3 beets, peeled & halved
- 1 tbsp olive oil
- 1 tsp sea salt
- 1 tsp balsamic vinegar
- ¼ cup goat cheese
- ¼ cup toasted walnuts

Instructions:

1. Toss beets with **olive oil and salt.**
2. Smoke at **225°F for 1 hour** until tender.
3. Slice and toss with **balsamic, goat cheese, and walnuts.**

Charcoal-Grilled Tandoori Paneer

Ingredients:

- 8 oz paneer, cubed
- ½ cup yogurt
- 1 tbsp lemon juice
- 1 tsp garam masala
- 1 tsp smoked paprika
- ½ tsp turmeric
- 1 tsp minced garlic

Instructions:

1. Mix marinade and coat paneer for **1 hour.**
2. Skewer and grill over **medium-high heat for 2-3 minutes per side.**

www.ingramcontent.com/pod-product-compliance
Lightning Source LLC
LaVergne TN
LVHW081459060526
838201LV00056BA/2829